THE SHAM

We all have the capac
In our increasing attu
have all become like shamans mapping our journeys and our relationships with Nature.

Shamanism is an ancient art, a creative craft, and a
way of wisdom, arising from the ages past to align
us with the transformative energies of Nature. To
follow the path of the Shaman, we need only open
our minds and our hearts to the wisdom surrounding us. Shamanism helps us connect—without
superstition and with sincerity—to Self, Nature,
and Spirit.

You have shamanic consciousness when you can
combine the focused awareness of waking consciousness with the unfocused flow of dreams,
inner vision, and non-waking consciousness. It is a
special altered state of consciousness in which you
are able to view your surroundings as a non-ordinary reality.

How you decide to adapt shamanic methods and
follow the path is your personal choice. We all have
the potential to be Aquarian shamans, reflecting
the coming of the Aquarian age. This book will
show you some of the tools and methods of
shamans past and present that you can incorporate
into your own personal blend of shamanic power.

About the Author

Amber Wolfe is a psychotherapist in private practice. She combines her 25 years of training in psychology, anthropology, and sociology with a lifetime of attunement to and study of the ways of Nature and Earth wisdom. Extensive travels gave Wolfe the opportunity to learn different cultures first hand. Like the shamans of old, she strives to "make her own medicine" by blending the wealth of wisdoms and experiences encountered on her life journey into a workable potion for psychological growth and spiritual development. She encourages all to follow their own paths to wisdom.

To Write to the Author

If you wish to contact the author or would like more information about this book, please write to the author in care of Llewellyn Worldwide and we will forward your request. Both the author and publisher appreciate hearing from you and learning of your enjoyment of this book and how it has helped you. Llewellyn Worldwide cannot guarantee that every letter written to the author can be answered, but all will be forwarded. Please write to:

Amber Wolfe
c/o Llewellyn Worldwide
P.O. Box 64383-889, St. Paul, MN 55164-0383, U.S.A.

Please enclose a self-addressed, stamped envelope for reply, or $1.00 to cover costs.
If outside U.S.A., enclose International postal reply coupon.

Free Catalog From Llewellyn

For more than 90 years Llewellyn has brought its readers knowledge in the fields of metaphysics and human potential. Learn about the newest books in spiritual guidance, natural healing, astrology, occult philosophy, and more. Enjoy book reviews, new age articles, a calender of events, plus current products and services. To get your free copy of *Llewellyn's New Worlds of Mind and Spirit*, send your name and address to:

Llewellyn's New Worlds of Mind and Spirit
P.O. Box 64383-889, St. Paul, MN 55164-0383, U.S.A.

LLEWELLYN'S VANGUARD SERIES

The Truth About

SHAMANISM

by Amber Wolfe

Author of
In the Shadow of the Shaman

1994
Llewellyn Publications,
St. Paul, MN 55164-0383, U.S.A.

The Truth About Shamanism. Copyright © 1988 by Llewellyn Publications. All rights reserved. Printed in the United States of America. No part of this book may be used or reproduced in any manner whatsoever without written permission from Llewellyn Publications except in the case of brief quotations embodied in critical articles and reviews.

For permission, or for serialization, condensation, or for adaptations, write the Publisher.

FIRST EDITION, 1988
SECOND EDITION
First Printing, 1994

International Standard Book Number:
0-87542-889-4

LLEWELLYN PUBLICATIONS
A Division of Llewellyn Worldwide, Ltd.
P.O. Box 64383, St. Paul, MN 55164-0383

Other Books by Amber Wolfe

In the Shadow of Shaman
Personal Alchemy

Llewellyn Publications is the oldest publisher of New Age Sciences in the Western Hemisphere. This book is one of a series of introductory explorations of each of the many fascinating dimensions of New Age Science—each important to a new understanding of Body and Soul, Mind and Spirit, of Nature and humanity's place in the world, and the vast unexplored regions of Microcosm and Macrocosm.

Please write for a full list of publications.

THE PATH OF THE SHAMAN
THEN AND NOW

I recently heard a wonderfully simple definition of the word *shaman*.

It was: "A shaman is one who helps people in their dealings with the other worlds."

These other worlds are the realms above, beyond, and deep within the experiences of our lives. These are the realms of spiritual, psychic vision and of pure, natural Earth energies. In shamanism, these worlds were traditionally represented as the upper world of the sky, or spirit levels, and the lower worlds of Earth and Nature. Humankind, along with all its symbols and traditions, was the middle world. Because of their abilities to alter their states of consciousness, the shamans was able to explore these worlds and bring back vision. The skill of the shamans was such that they could interpret the contents of their vision for the people.

One of the ancient symbols representing the shaman was that of the living tree. This symbolized the shaman as a rooted, living channel between sky and Earth, between Humankind and Spirit. Because of the shamans' great connectedness to the chaotic energies of Nature and Spirit, they were the journey-makers between the worlds. Only the shaman was considered able to control the flow of energies in the other worlds. This ability came from the many lessons and experiences that were part and parcel of the shamanic path. These varied experiences gave the shaman the wisdom, perspective and objectivity to work with all the worlds of Nature, Spirit, and Humankind. The shaman was master of energies beyond the understanding of most other people.

Often, the methods for making these otherworldly journeys were kept secret and hidden from the people. The knowledge gained from the shaman's journeys was rationed out to selected students and initiates who were considered ready for the experience of otherworldly journeys. The work and methods of the shaman were jealously guarded in some cultures, leaving no access to the knowledge for the people they served. However, there were some shamans who endeavored to do more than just interpret their own experiences in the journeys to other worlds. These shamans returned from their journeys with psychic methods, maps, and guidelines to help the people gain their own knowledge.

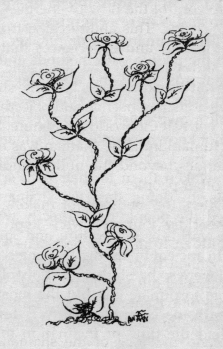

These shaman mapmakers had perhaps learned one of the deepest wisdoms of shamanism:

There are no other journeys than the journey of the Self. Each person must make his (or her) own journey in this world or that within—the realms of everyday or within those of spiritual vision and Nature's energies.

The shaman, as mapmaker, could assist the people with methods and point out hazards along the way. The shaman could even summon forth aspects of the people's own spirit and power that they had not known existed. The shaman could evoke the highest abilities of the people and awaken them to their own spiritual quests. In doing this, the shaman truly helped the people deal directly with the other worlds of Self, Nature, and Spirit.

In ancient times, the challenges to survival were so harsh that most people were unable to pursue any but the most basic life paths necessary to live. Very few people had the time or inclination to make explorative journeys into Spirit or to consider the subtle balance of energies in Nature. Nature was sometimes adversary, sometimes nurturer; always Mother—Core of all life. Primitive people looked to the shaman to interpret the surrounding mysteries of Nature and to communicate with the realms of Spirit. The shamans were protected, honored, and often feared by the people for the powers they held.

While the role of the shaman was central to the life of the people, the presence of the shaman was often quite separate from them. The shaman had abilities and wisdom that clearly set them apart. Additionally, the levels of openness and attunement to the energies of Nature that the shaman had to maintain, made it difficult to live among others. One meaning of the word shaman is "ascetic." Ascetic means someone who chooses to live a life of self-denial and isolation, generally in the service of a higher cause.

At times, the isolation of the shaman required another person of wisdom to act as an intermediary between the shaman and the people. Most often this was a medicine person whose knowledge and experience closely paralleled those of the shaman. While the shaman some- times chose to live apart from the people, the medicine person lived within the center of the community. Indeed, the medicine person was seen as the core of the tribe or community. Although the shaman was an object of awe and sometimes fear, the medicine person was a comfortable, familiar part of the community.

Many traditions held that the shamans had suffered self-inflicted mortal wounds, or had been devoured by the spirits and energies of the other worlds. The shaman had endured these traumas, returning wounded, yet self-healed. These experiences gave the shaman the great compassion and sensitivity of a wounded healer. The shaman had experienced the horrors and healings of the other world. As wounded healer, the shaman dwelt between the worlds, ready to travel into Spirit at all times to facilitate healing for another person.

The shamans knew that their function was to remain as a clear connection to the other worlds and as a centering force for the chaotic energies surrounding Humankind. The shaman's task was to stay centered in self-power, uninfluenced by the paths of others. Differences in traditions and philosophies meant nothing to the shamans. The energies they held, and the levels they dwelt upon, were beyond division. While the shamans reflected the myth and tradition of their people, their not ruled by these. The shaman held the boundless, purest forms of Nature energy. "When shamans healed someone, they dealt directly with the necessary energies. they pulled these through themselves and through the patient. The healing process was, and is, completely cooperative and interactive. To ignore the contribution of either is to miss the beautiful dance of shamanic healing.

The shaman knew that just as all paths are self-paths, all healings are self-healings. In the presence of the shaman, the person could often release the blocks and doubts that prevented him or her from reaching the deepest levels of wisdom and self-healing. Most people, particularly in ancient times, considered the healings to be only the magical actions of the shaman. When patients had other world experiences during a shamanic healing, they most probably did not consider them to be self experiences. More likely, they considered them to be the magic of the shaman.

All of the tools, props, and ornamentations of the shamans did little to convince the person of their own self-healing abilities. However, what these did was to open the levels of faith needed to let healing energies through. Simply put, faith-healing is self-healing. The shaman, as wounded healer, was, and is, most purely a self-healer. The shamans' tools were the symbolic connections they had made to the deep healing levels and to Nature energies. These tools were their totems and sacred helpers. They were the link to the powers and worlds beyond form. They mapped the way and enabled the shaman to meet, Spirit to Spirit, with the person being healed. With such a meeting of Spirits, the possibilities for healing and transformations were limitless.

They still are.

As we have evolved in modern times, we have become much more conscious of our incredible self-healing abilities. We have begun to access the vast amounts of knowledge stored in the other world aspects of our Self. Like the shaman of old, we have become aware of ourselves at the center of a great cosmic dance of worlds, energies and Spirit in Nature. Shamanism, as we explore it today, maps the way to the worlds of Nature in order to help us grow and expand our own vision.

We all have the capacities to follow a shamanic path. In our increasing attunement to Earth wisdom, we have all become like shamans mapping our journeys and our relationships with Nature. Upper, lower, middle, and Spirit worlds blend as we dance with Nature and with our Self. Our expanding awareness and relationships to the worlds of minerals, plants, humans, and animals have become central to our greater communion with Nature.

As we move closer to the center of our Self, we see that all of the wisdom and experiences of our lives have been like a great shamanic journey. Whatever traditions or philosophies we have explored before beginning our study of shamanism may be seen as part of the journey, or path, of the Self. The path of the shaman is truly the path of the Self.

In the reemergence of interest in shamanism, we can all learn from the wisdom and energies of Nature. The abilities shown by the shamans can be, and are being, awakened in all of us who wish to tap directly into the heart of Earth wisdom and spiritual vision. We are ready for a more significant communion with the other world aspects of our Self and with the purest energy of Nature. The shamanic path gives us this clearly by demonstrating the remarkable gifts of power and attunement that we may attain, for the good of all.

The path of the shaman is a constantly moving, changing dance of life. Everything in the shaman's universe has energy, vibration, consciousness, and power of its own. This view of the universe is called animism. The quest of the shamanic path is to achieve attunement with these vibrations and familiarity with Spirit. This level of attunement and familiarity represents the attainment of power for the shaman.

Even in the attainment of this power and the mastery of these vibrations and energies, the shaman knows that power is a gift. Whatever has or has not been done in pursuit of this power, it is ultimately a gift of Spirit to Self. Knowing this, shamans can allow the energies of all the worlds about them to flow through. *The shaman stands at the center of all the worlds, balanced and in harmony with life. This is the heart of the Shamanic Path.*

I've spent the last few pages discussing the traditional views of the shaman and the shamanic path for several reasons. One reason is that the reemergence of interest in shamanism has made the word shaman far more common than the person of the shaman, who is always a rare, special individual. Another reason is that many of the historical hallmarks of the shaman can provide guidelines for us in present times. Finally, by understanding how the shaman has been viewed in ancient times, we can begin to see how far we have come in both our present view of shamanism and our self-view as well.

When we understand the heart of the shamanic path, we may be better able to see how we can incorporate shamanic methods and experiences into our own self-development. An added benefit is that our development parallels the development of the planet. As we grow in strength and power, we empower the planet and all who live here. *Our attunement to the deep shamanic energies of Nature heals and nurtures Nature itself.*

Heal yourself—Heal Mother Earth

LAKOTA WISDOM

One of the most beautiful, synchronous aspects of the current shamanic reemergence is that it coincides with the great expansion in human consciousness and potential. The shamans of old may have had to rely on harsh experiences of physical and psychic trauma to access and tune into other worlds beyond form. We, however, have now reached a place in human development that allows us to delve into the deepest wisdom and purest form of energy.

The methods used by shamans of old may now be adapted for our lives today. Instead of a rare few individuals undergoing the rigors of ancient shamanic methods, we can be many, gently stretching and experiencing our new-found potentials. We can all attune to the center of our Self, lovingly reconnecting with Spirit, with Nature, and with the intricate interweavings of life.

We find harmony with all the energies of Nature and Spirit by opening ourselves to experience fully *all* that is around us. The shamanic view portrays all aspects of life as wheels within wheels, spinning and turning constantly. When we follow a shamanic path, we reach into this seemingly chaotic universe of spinning wheels. With our personal faith and willingness, we connect with each wheel individually. Each experience of our life, each aspect of Nature, and each journey of Spirit we may see as a wheel.

The larger wheels of the Animal, Plant, Mineral, and Human Worlds contain smaller wheels of specific lessons and connections to power. The great wheels of the elements: Air, Fire, Water, and Earth, we find spinning in and out of all the worlds. Spirit we find throughout all, supporting our quest on the shamanic path. Like the shaman, we connect with the *All* of the universe by first connecting with each aspect individually. This is called riding the wheel of life. As we do this, we find different parts of each wheel, and different vibrations of energy which help us stay in balance.

We ride at the center of the wheel of life when we follow the shamanic path. At the center of the wheel, we find that the source of all the wheels we ride, the source of the energies we encounter, and the source of the journey we are on, is our highest Self. *Journeys of upper, lower, and middle worlds are journeys of Self. When we know that, we are able to transform the very wheel of life that we ride.*

Like the shamans of old, we may make the quest of attunement with all worlds and harmony with Spirit. Beyond that, when we ride the wheels of our life in balance, we help balance everything else. Everything. But first we begin with one aspect of Self, one element, one part of Nature, one world——one wheel at a time. And so we go, from wheel to wheel, all spinning within the great wheel of life. This continues until we have dealt (conceivably) with them all. Then, we start again. For the shaman, like the Fool in the Tarot deck, is always at the beginning of his path. To forget that is to lose the balanced flow of energies which keeps the follower of the shamanic path centered in his own power.

Fortunately, each journey, each turn of the wheel, gives us wisdom and experience to facilitate the next. Now, more than ever before in human evolution, we have the resources and abilities to support our journey on the shamanic path. Each journey and each experience we encounter is deeper and swifter than before. As we spiral into the shamanic center of Self, we find that the energies often bring radical changes and personal transformations in our lives. This is why we take the time to connect individually with each aspect of our journey on the shamanic path. This we do well, and in balance. This is also why we learn to call on all the resources around us, and within us, for strength and support along the way. We learn to use our own blends of power and gifts to map our shamanic path and to make each step of our Earth walk true and sure.

How we decide to adapt shamanic methods and follow a shamanic path is our personal choice. From the shamans of old, we may now take the great wisdom of staying centered in our own power. We take the isolation of the shaman and translate it into inner solitude. The traumas and woundings of the shaman we find already in our own life experiences. We reach into our own hearts and find the compassion of the wounded healer. For who among us has lived untouched by pain or pleasure? The shaman's experiences of being devoured and reemerging from the brink of death we may find in the deep personal transformation of our own Being. To choose to follow a shamanic path is to call for healing and transformation from the deepest center of our Self. From this center we are most connected to the purest energies of all, the worlds of Self, Nature, and Spirit.

From the shamans of old, we learn to develop our shamanic self, egocentric in the most positive sense and centered in personal power. We walk our own paths. We may choose to live an isolated life, defining ourselves as shamans in the old way, with all that path entails. Or we may decide to live closer to the center of our own community and to the world community. This way we are following the tradition of the medicine person who always dwells within the community as an active participant.

In this time of blending philosophies, we may follow a shamanic path and still function as a medicine person. In blending these together, we may find that the deep self-healing experiences of the shamanic path can provide the necessary strength for the medicine person. The medicine person is often depleted by the task of serving at the center of the community, which has its own chaotic energies. On the other hand, the strict shamanic follower who may have become too isolated along the path may find the energies of a community to have positive contributions to his/her own self-healing. Shamanic paths, like all personal paths, can run parallel or across the paths of others while remaining deeply personal and individual. We may use symbols and philosophies from many different sources, blending them to "make our own medicine" on the shamanic path.

We may call ourselves by any name, or follow any tradition, and still be on a shamanic path—*so long as we are walking connected and in balance with the energies of Nature.*

We may be Wiccan, Buddhist, Taoist, Christian, or Hindu and enter into shamanism. Nature is everywhere, and the energies are shared by all. We have the capacities to be Aquarian shamans, reflecting the blending of the Aquarian age. This we do by creating our own journey and combining our many experiences and philosophies together into a workable whole.

With our increased potentials and awareness, we have a greater wealth of resources available. The resources we call on now come from a wider range of shared wisdom and expanded consciousness, which the shaman of old could only have glimpsed in during individual journeys of time and space.

Perhaps these old shamans did more than merely glimpse the future in which we find ourselves now. Perhaps they did see the great blending of wisdom and philosophies that mark the new Aquarian age. Perhaps they saw the consciousness of Humankind expanding at a rate beyond our capacities to measure it. Perhaps they felt the neurons firing in each individual brain, creating new pathways in the Mind of us all. Perhaps they felt the great wave of Spiritual oneness, unity, and Nature awareness sweep over us, stirring long-forgotten memories deep within us.

Perhaps, then, these shamans of old knew that all they had endured had been worthwhile. For they had glimpsed a new age of humanity arriving on the planet. They had seen the many, not the few, who came ready and equipped to explore the other worlds that the shamans had endured so much to reach. Perhaps these old shamans laughed to see us struggle with their ancient wisdom, like babies first crawling from the crib. Perhaps they felt some fleeting sadness as we examined their tools of power as scientists, as anthropologists, and finally as students.

Perhaps when they glimpsed us taking our first uncertain steps on the shamanic path, these old shamans called together all of their helping spirits and returned to their places of isolation. There, they called together the energies of Nature and Spirit, and let them flow through—across time and space—to direct us on our journey as a people and as a planet.

ASPECTS OF SHAMANISM

I. Power Object

It has been said, power is effective energy. In the shamanic philosophy all aspects of the universe have energy, which has potential use and power. Developing a relationship with objects in Nature, or in Spirit, to use their energy is called developing a totemic relationship. Power objects are totems for the shaman.

It is important to remember that power is not confined in an object. The power of any totem comes from the trusting, interactive relationship between the object and the shaman. Of all power objects, the shaman knows that the Self is the most sacred. *Totems provide a symbolic link between the shaman and the highest aspects of Self, Nature, and Spirit.*

Power objects are found in a variety of ways. Most often, objects such as rocks, feathers, herbs, or other items from Nature appear in a way that seems special, unusual, or meaningful to the follower of the shamanic path. An object that has potential as a totem will make you feel strongly attracted to it. Like people of kindred spirits, the shaman and the totems are drawn together.

In the case of power animals, sometimes called allies, the first connection is often made in a dream or a meditative state of consciousness. It is an old tradition in shamanism, that an object which has true totemic potential must reveal itself in four different ways to the follower of the shamanic path. These ways may include dreams, visions, gifts, Nature encounters, and showing up in unexpected places. The key is that the attraction between the object and the person is strong, positive, and immediate.

Another way to develop totemic relationships is to examine connections you have already made with an object or spirit. To deepen this connection and to initiate trusting communication, you may perform a gentle ceremony to help strengthen your ties with the object. A simple ceremony can consist of "honoring the directions" by calling in the energies and attributes of each direction: South, West, North, and East. This is done to bless and awaken the effective totem energies in the power object. A simple form of this ceremony is given below:

POWER OBJECT CEREMONY

Draw a circle clockwise (either real or imaginary). Step inside the circle.

Hold the power object, if you can, or place it inside the circle with you. If the object is a spirit guide or power animal spirit, hold it in your imagination, or bring something to represent it, such as a figurine.

Stand facing South.

South represents the attributes of faith, strength, and protection that your relationship with the power object can bring to you.

Imagine the energies of faith, strength, and protection flowing into the circle, into your power object, and into yourself.

Give thanks and honor to the energies of the South.

Next, turn to your right and face West.

West represents the attributes of inner vision, self-healing, and balance which your power object may help you develop.

Imagine yourself opening to the attributes of inner vision, self-healing, and balance.

Feel the energies of these attributes flow into the circle, into your power object, and into yourself.

Give thanks and honor the energies of the West.

Next, turn to your right and stand facing North.

North represents the attributes of wisdom, practicality, and patience.

Imagine yourself connecting to the attributes of wisdom, practicality, and patience. Feel the energies of these attributes flow into the circle, into your power object, and into yourself.

Give thanks and honor the energies of the North.

Next turn to your right and stand facing East.

East represents the attributes of creativity, illumination, and perception.

Imagine yourself receiving the attributes of creativity, illumination, and perception. Feel the energies of these attributes flow into the circle, into your power object, and into yourself.

Give thanks and honor the energies of the East.

Now turn right once again and stand facing South where you began.

You have completed a full circle of energies and attributes to use in your relationship with your power object and in your relationship with your Self.

Now look *upward* to symbolize the shamanic connection you are making with the upper world of spiritual, psychic vision.

Imagine a pathway between yourself and the energies of Spirit. Extend that pathway to connect with your power object. Feel the energies of Spirit flowing down into the circle, into your power object, and into your Self.

Give thanks and honor the energies of the Spirit.

Now look *downward* to symbolize the shamanic connection you are making with the lower world of Earth energies.

Imagine a rooted connection between yourself and the energies of Earth. Extend that rooted connection to include your power object. Feel the energies of Earth flowing upward into your circle, into your power object, and into yourself.

Still facing South where you began, hold your power object close to your heart, or imagine it within your heart.

Feel all of the energies and attributes of all the directions flow into your heart— through your power object.

From the South, feel faith, strength, and protection.

From the West, feel inner vision, self-healing, and balance.

From the North, feel wisdom, practicality, and patience.

From the East, feel creativity, illumination, and perception.

From above, feel the high energy of Spirit.

From below, feel the supportive energy of Earth.

From within yourself, feel a new connection to all the directions and worlds of Self, Nature, and Spirit.

Know that your power object has become a symbolic link between yourself and the positive energies surrounding you.

Give thanks and honor all of the energies that support and strengthen you on your shamanic path.

The ceremony is completed.

Step out of the circle. Walk in balance.

When you do a simple ceremony such as the one above, you are symbolizing yourself on the shamanic path. **The circle represents yourself in the center of all the universe. By pulling in the energies of all the directions, as well as those of Spirit and Earth, you are balancing your personal**

power. A ceremony such as this may be adapted to use with or without a power object. It can be used to help you stay centered in personal power, connected to the energies of the universe around and within you.

II. Shamanic Consciousness

To understand the sacred, other world journey of the shaman, it is necessary to first understand shamanic consciousness. To begin with, consciousness is usually divided into two primary types:

1. The focused, waking consciousness in which we are alert and aware of our surroundings

2. The unfocused, non-waking consciousness in which we are either dreaming or unconscious of our surroundings.

Simply put, shamanic consciousness blends the focused awareness of waking consciousness with the unfocused flow of dreams, inner vision, and non-waking consciousness.

Although the sacred, other worlds of the shamans are sometimes called dream worlds or dream time, the shamanic state of consciousness is much more focused and alert than dreams. It is because of this special state of shamanic consciousness that the shaman can interpret and interact with the visionary contents of journeys to other worlds.

Shamanic consciousness is a special altered state of consciousness in which the shaman is able to view close surroundings as a non-ordinary reality. The shaman is aware of the concrete levels of reality that include the everyday world of Humankind. The shaman is also aware of the abstract world of Nature energies and Spirit.

Shamanic consciousness allows the shaman to be aware of all levels or worlds at the same time. This is what is meant by saying the shaman exists between the worlds. For the shaman, both the concrete and the abstract levels have significance, meaning, and validity. The shaman has the ability to draw information and wisdom from all levels, and the abilities to not confuse them with each other

Some modern psychologists and scientists have regarded the other world journeys of the shamans as a kind of mental delusion. However, it is the clear ability of the shaman to separate the concrete and abstract, while still gaining wisdom from all levels, that sets the experience well apart from a mental delusion. The shaman has psychic objectivity, which facilitates interpretations of visions and other world journeys. This is done to find the message of significance for the shaman's work.

Other psychologists have recognized the uniqueness of shamanic consciousness and have sought to develop forms of therapy based on ancient shamanic methods. One of the most familiar forms of this is guided imagery, also called active imagery. Because of the active and interactive involvement of the shaman, the experience of the other world journeys may be closely related to the active use of imagery. Basically, a shamanic journey can be considered to be a very special form of self-guided imagery. Or, perhaps it would be more appropriate to say imagery guided by the highest aspect of Self. It is the shaman's diligent exploration of mind consciousness that enables other world journeys and return with wisdom for his/her own path and for others.

Carl Jung, the great Western psychoanalyst and mystic, once compared the mind of man to a large apartment building. While most people in an apartment building are familiar with a few floors and a few other residents of the building, very few know them all. The shaman, as an explorer and experimenter in mind and consciousness, strives to "visit all the floors and residents and return home without getting lost." This sense of exploration and experimentation is the heart of the sacred, shamanic journey. By making these explorative journeys, the shaman becomes the channel between the worlds of Self, Nature, and Spirit.

Like a living tree, the shaman is rooted in concrete consciousness while reaching into abstract consciousness. We can carry this ancient analogy of the shaman as a living tree further. The trunk of the tree can represent the shaman in relation to the middle world of Humankind—as well as the connected channel between the upper and lower worlds. The deepest roots can represent the pure energies of Nature encountered on Earth journeys. The highest limbs can represent the shaman reaching into the upper astral aspects of Spirit encountered on Vision Quests. Where the roots of the tree meet the ground can represent the strength and balance needed by the shaman to stay centered in personal power

When followers of the shamanic path begin to explore mind and consciousness by making other world journeys, the symbol of the shaman as the living tree is a solid reminder of the kind of balance and connectedness needed to have effective, positive results.

In order to make other world journeys, shamans often use several different methods to achieve a deeper state of shamanic consciousness. This is sometimes called "reaching the journey levels." In some traditions, these methods included forced trance, strict deprivation, and hallucinogens. The harshness of these methods reflects the attitude of some shamans that the other worlds are filled with danger and terror. It is felt that the shaman has to be extremely careful to avoid peril. This view has been called "the Way of the Warrior" to symbolize the battle attitude of the shaman.

Other traditions hold the view that life is a series of interweavings and creations, of which the other world journeys are an exciting and integral part. This view has been called the "Way of the Adventurer." Interestingly, the Way of the Adventurer invovles very gentle methods of relaxation and mental imagery to enter the journey levels. Both traditions use drums, rattles, and other simple musical instruments to create a steady rhythm that enhances their abilities to reach shamanic journey levels of consciousness.

It is certainly possible to blend aspects of both basic traditions to create your own methods of achieving shamanic journey levels. From the Way of the Warrior, we can take the harshness and translate it into a seriousness of mind and attitude about our explorations into consciousness. The perils and dangers we can see as a wise reminder to be gentle with ourselves and cautious of our own power and energies. The Warrior we can transform into a Spiritual Warrior striving for wisdom, awareness, and self-healing by using positive methods and attitudes for the good of all.

From the Way of the Adventurer, we can take the joy of life experience and create our own paths. Through the use of gentle mental imagery we can see as the use of our increased brain and mind potentials. As a follower of a shamanic path, we can experience life as a spiritual adventurer, moving to a rhythm of our own creation.

In explaining the levels of shamanic consciousness, or in making journeys to the other worlds, it is wise for the follower of the shamanic path to *remember that the shaman seeks to be connected to the Earth, not detached from it.*

III. Shamanic Healing

Shamanic healings have long been shrouded in mystery, misunderstanding, and superstition. Still, as we learn to better understand the shamanic philosophy of life, we can begin to have clarity about this special form of healing. Basically, the shaman views the purpose of life as being spiritual development and attunement. This attainment means that the individual spirit, or soul, is in harmony with all the aspects of Self, Nature, and Spirit.

A healthy soul, or spirit, is one who maintains a balanced relationship with all of the energies of the universe. The attunement of Mind, Body, and Spirit is seen to be a harmonious quest, resulting in both health and wholeness.

The shamanic concepts of a web of life, a net of power, or a fabric of existence shared by all, reflects the recognition of the complex interweavings of energies that is the universe. For the shaman, there is no real separation of Mind, Body, and Spirit— no separation of the worlds or levels of consciousness other than ones that are arbitrarily created to give us individual identity and form. Each individual is viewed as a thread in a great universal tapestry, woven with a harmonious living pattern. So long as an individual is on a balance path, the thread that the individual represents runs true. When an imbalance occurs for the individual, then disharmony, or disease, occurs.

The sick or diseased person is viewed as having a disorder of Spirit that has interfered with natural attunement to the energies of the universe. This lack of attunement is seen as having caused a loss of power, or a hole in the protective mantle of energies surrounding the individual. These holes further cause damage to the universal fabric of life.

Like the proverbial weak link in a chain, the sick person is seen as a single link that must be dealt with in order to maintain the strength of the whole. This strengthening, or healing process, is done to realign the individual with all the energies of the universe. For this reason, the first order of business in shamanic healing is to increase the power of the sick person. In order to facilitate healing for the sick person, the shaman must first strive to mend the leaks of personal power. Only then can the power of the disease be dealt with effectively.

In both stages of shamanic healing—the strengthening of personal power, and the counter actions against the power of the illness—the shaman uses methods and medicines designed to encourage the sick person (Body, Mind, and Spirit) to participate in the healing process. **The shaman enters the realm of journey-level con-**

sciousness and active imagination in order to share the experience of the disease and of the healing. The shaman, as master of energies and evoker of imagery, can catalyze or facilitate the healing process of the individual.

In shamanic healing, both the shaman and the sick person share the view of the interconnectedness of all aspects of life. The task of the shaman is to make the sick person fully aware of the significance and meaning of the disease. This awareness goes beyond physical and mental awareness into spiritual understanding of the cause and effect of the disease. Again, the shaman views disease as a disorder of Spirit.

In the shamanic healing process, the shaman and the sick person share a level of awareness at which they are able to communicate, Spirit to Spirit. At this level of awareness, the sick person is able to choose to become healthy by redirecting inner energies, realigning with those of the universe. But most importantly, the sick person must be the one to choose this. For just as the shaman makes no value distinction between the worlds of Self, Nature, and Spirit, the shaman makes no value distinction between life and death. Both are viewed as part of the same process of spiritual attunement and development.

It may be clearer to say that the shaman makes no value judgment in the healing process. Life and death are seen as equally valuable resolutions in the process of re-aligning the individual with Spirit. Where and how the sick person chooses to realign with Spirit is seen as an individual choice to make—not the shaman's.

It is natural that this attitude is greatly misunderstood—particularly in Western society, which views the healing process in terms of success and failure.

Shamanic healing may be best viewed as a process of awareness of choice. The outcome is viewed as a choice made, rather than a success or failure on the part of the sick person or the shaman.

The shaman works to remove all obstacles to clarity and to mend leaks of personal power, in order to let the sick person's natural self-healing process work its own wonders. Whatever the methods used or the medicine applied, *the shaman knows that these only serve to clear the path for the process of self-healing, which must ultimately take over.*

Tales of shamans removing masses of disease and tumors from a sick person's body are, more often than not, symbolic and ritualistic removals of other substituted objects. These symbolic rituals are used to represent the ability of the shaman, in unity with the ability of the sick person, to remove the actual disease. These rituals should not be viewed as tricks, but as tools that focus the sick person's awareness on the process of self-healing.

As to the documented cases of actual physical removal of diseased tumors and growths from the body of the sick person: scientists are striving to find a framework in which to understand, explain, or measure the process. Although such cases are exceedingly rare, they do exist and they do defy conventional measurement or definition. It may be that the interactive healing process of the shaman and the self-healing of the sick person reaches a level we can only speculate on metaphysically.

Perhaps it is best to approach such phenomena in shamanic healing by remembering one thing: **The shaman seeks clarification—not verification**. However strange a shamanic healing process may seem, it is the clear function of the healing process we must seek. If the function is to help the individual find clarity and awareness of his or her own self-healing abilities, then the function is positive. If the function is to amaze others with immeasurable feats and phenomenal actions, then the function is in danger of becoming negative.

The process of self-healing is an incredibly complex issue. It is one that we will continue to be enlightened about as we evolve in our own ability and perceptions. For followers of a shamanic path, the incredible "miracles" of the shamans may best be seen as reminders and symbols of our own self-healing abilities. It is also useful to remember that self-healing comes from the working connection of Body, Mind, and Spirit. **To truly understand and experience shamanic healing, we must first seek to align and attune our own energies of Mind/Body/Spirit**. From this alignment and attunement we may begin to glimpse the powers of shamanic self-healing.

IV. Shamanic Symbols

Functioning as a priest(ess), healer and channel between the worlds, the shaman calls on a very unique abilities—that of divination. Divination is the ability to use perception and attunement to interpret signs and symbols. Shamanic divination is most closely related to the modern processes of diagnosis as used by doctors and analysis as used by psychologists. Just as doctors use physical symptoms to identify an illness and psychologists use behaviors to identify a disordered state of mind, the shaman uses signs from all aspects of Body/Mind/Spirit and Nature to identify surrounding conditions for people. The healing process of modern medicine and psychology involves a period of diagnosis before treatment. In much the same way, the work of the shaman requires the process of divination in order to deal with the energies of Nature and the realms of Spirit.

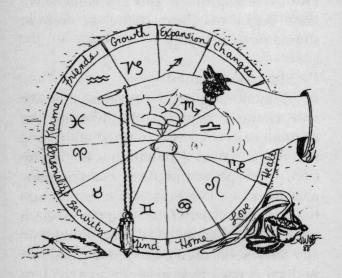

Many modern forms of divination have evolved into complicated and intricate systems, such as Tarot decks and astrology. These divination systems, like many others, can trace their origins to shamanic roots. However, their symbolic complexities have carried them somewhat away from the upper and lower worlds of the shaman, and have left them more in the middle world realm of Humankind. The unique form of shamanic divination is based on interpreting Nature aspects. The Plant, Animal, Mineral, and Human worlds are interpreted directly by the shaman. Their natural attributes symbolize similar qualities in the shaman and in the people.

For example: An eagle seen circling the community, then flying toward a distant mountain may be interpreted by the shaman to mean a time of spiritual healing is needed. This interpretation, or divination, from Nature signs is based on the shaman's observance of the event and on his wisdom of what each aspect symbolized. The eagle, because it flies higher than any other bird, is thought to represent the highest forms of power. The eagle flies closest to the upper world of Spirit, so its power is spiritual. That which is closest to Spirit is most healing, therefore the eagle represents spiritual healing. Because the eagle circled the community, it may be interpreted that the need is for group spiritual healing. That the eagle flew off toward a distant mountain may be interpreted as a need for the shaman to go to the mountain and bring back spiritual healing to the community. Or it may be interpreted as symbolizing the need for the community to climb higher into spiritual awareness through ceremony or ritual.

Shamanic divination is not like an exact science with predictable causes and effects. The task of the shaman, in interpreting symbols from Nature, is to be flexible and continually open to new signs and information.

Because of the shamanic view of the living, vibrational interrelationships of all aspects of life, symbols from Nature can speak clearly to those who are attuned to it. As we in modern times begin to reclaim our connections to Nature, we are able to hear the messages it brings us. In the days when Humankind felt itself somehow separate from Nature, those who "watched for signs" were often ridiculed. Now, however, more and more of us are realizing that our relationship to Nature is deeply personal and significant in our lives. Whether we feel a strong connection to a part of Nature, or whether something from Nature appears to us in dreams or from an unusual source, we have begun to seek its meaning for us. This is the heart of shamanic divination.

Although many signs and events in Nature have come to have traditional symbolic meanings, it is our personal interpretation that we learn to look for first. All of the significant signs and events in Self, Nature, and Spirit are there to help the follower of the shamanic path If what we divine, or interpret, has meaning for another, it is because their path led them to it.

Like the shaman of old, we may be a catalyst to growth and knowledge, so long as we don't seek to force our meanings or our paths on others. The shaman shares knowledge but does not seek to own it. For knowledge is power, and power is a gift.

Shamanism is an ancient art, a creative craft, and a way of wisdom arising from the ages past to align us with the transformative energies of Nature. To follow the path of the shaman, we need only open our minds and our hearts to the wisdom surrounding us. Shamanism helps us explore, and connect without superstition but with sincerity, to Self, Nature, and Spirit.

STAY IN TOUCH

On the following pages you will find some of the books now available on related subjects. Your book dealer stocks most of these and will stock new titles in the Llewellyn series as they become available. We urge your patronage.

To obtain our full catalog write for our bimonthly news magazine/catalog, *Llewellyn's New Worlds of Mind and Spirit*. A sample copy is free, and it will continue coming to you at no cost as long as you are an active mail customer. Or you may subscribe for just $10.00 in the U.S.A. and Canada ($20.00 overseas, first class mail). Many bookstores also have *New Worlds* available to their customers. Ask for it.

Llewellyn's New Worlds of Mind and Spirit
P.O. Box 64383-889, St. Paul, MN 55164-0383, U.S.A.

TO ORDER BOOKS AND TAPES

If your book dealer does not have the books described, you may order them directly from the publisher by sending full price in U.S. funds, plus $3.00 for postage and handling for orders under $10.00; $4.00 for orders *over* $10.00. There are no postage and handling charges for orders over $50.00. Postage and handling rates are subject to change. We ship UPS whenever possible. Delivery guaranteed. Provide your street address as UPS does not deliver to P.O. Boxes. UPS to Canada requires a $50.00 minimum order. Allow 4-6 weeks for delivery. Orders outside the U.S.A. and Canada: Airmail—add retail price of book; add $5.00 for each non-book item (tapes, etc.); add $1.00 per item for surface mail. Mail orders to:

LLEWELLYN PUBLICATIONS
P.O. BOX 64383-889, St. Paul, MN 55164-0383, U.S.A.

Prices subject to change without notice.

BY OAK, ASH & THORN
Modern Celtic Shamanism
by D. J. Conway

Many spiritual seekers are interested in shamanism because it is a spiritual path that can be followed in conjunction with any religion or other spiritual belief without conflict. Shamanism has not only been practiced by Native American and African cultures—for centuries, it was practiced by the Europeans, including the Celts.

By Oak, Ash and Thorn presents a workable, modern form of Celtic shamanism that will help anyone broaden spiritual awareness. Here, in simple, practical terms, you will learn to follow specific exercises and apply techniques that will develop your spiritual awareness and ties with the natural world: shape-shifting, divination by the Celtic Ogham alphabet, Celtic shamanic tools, traveling to and using magick in the three realms of the Celtic other worlds, empowering the self, journeying through meditation and more.

Shamanism begins as a personal revelation and inner healing, then evolves into a striving to bring balance and healing into the Earth itself. This book will ensure that Celtic shamanism will take its place among the spiritual practices that help us lead fuller lives.

ISBN: 1-56718-166-X, 6 x 9, est. 288 pp., illus., sftcvr. $12.95

IN THE SHADOW OF THE SHAMAN
by Amber Wolfe

Presented in what the author calls a "cookbook shamanism" style, *In the Shadow of the Shaman* shares recipes, ingredients, and methods of preparation for experiencing some very ancient wisdom—wisdoms of Native American and Wiccan traditions, as well as contributions from other philosophies of Nature, as they are used in the shamanic way. Wolfe encourages us to feel confident and free to use her methods to cook up something new, completely on our own. This blending of ancient formulas and personal methods represents what Ms. Wolfe calls Aquarian Shamanism.

Along with increased interest in shamanic way—the deep, direct ways of Nature there have also come many people who urge us to follow a certain set method to attune to shamanic energies. In this book you are encouraged to be ever mindful of your truest teacher, the guide within. Wolfe encourages you to follow that wisdom that dwells within your center. When you do this, you are following the heart of the shamanic path; and this makes us open to the wonderful, pure energies of Nature.

In the Shadow of the Shaman is designed to communicate in the most practical, direct ways possible, so that the wisdom and the energy may be shared for the benefit of all. Whatever your system or tradition, you will find *In the Shadow of the Shaman* a valuable book, a resource, a friend, a gentle guide and support on your journey. Dancing in the shadow of the shaman, you will find new dimensions of Spirit.

0-87542-888-6, 6 x 9, illus., 350 pages **$12.95**

IN THE SHADOW OF THE SHAMAN
by Amber Wolfe

Presented in what the author calls a "cookbook shaman-ism" style, *In the Shadow of the Shaman* shares recipes, ingredients, and methods of preparation for experiencing some very ancient wisdom—wisdoms of Native Ameri-can and Wiccan traditions, as well as contributions from other philosophies of Nature, as they are used in the shamanic way. Wolfe encourages us to feel confident and free to use her methods to cook up something new, com-pletely on our own. This blending of ancient formulas and personal methods represents what Ms. Wolfe calls Aquarian Shamanism.

Along with increased interest in shamanic way—the deep, direct ways of Nature there have also come many people who urge us to follow a certain set method to attune to shamanic energies. In this book you are encour-aged to be ever mindful of your truest teacher, the guide within. Wolfe encourages you to follow that wisdom that dwells within your center. When you do this, you are fol-lowing the heart of the shamanic path; and this makes us open to the wonderful, pure energies of Nature.

In the Shadow of the Shaman is designed to communicate in the most practical, direct ways possible, so that the wisdom and the energy may be shared for the benefit of all. Whatever your system or tradition, you will find *In the Shadow of the Shaman* a valuable book, a resource, a friend, a gentle guide and support on your journey. Dancing in the shadow of the shaman, you will find new dimensions of Spirit.

0-87542-888-6, 6 x 9, illus., 350 pages $12.95

PERSONAL ALCHEMY
A Handbook of Healing & Self-Transformation
by Amber Wolfe

Personal Alchemy offers the first bold look at the practical use of "Rays" for healing and self-development. Rays are spontaneous energy emanations emitting a specific quality, property or attribute. The Red Ray, for example, represents the energies of life force, survival and strength. When used in conjunction with active imagery, the alchemical properties of the Red Ray can activate independence, release inferiority, or realign destructiveness and frustration. *Personal Alchemy* explains each color Ray and Light in depth, in a manner designed to teach the material and to encourage the active participation of the reader.

What's more, this book goes beyond anything else written on the Rays because it contains an extensive set of alchemical correlations that amplify the Ray's powers. Each Ray correlates with a specific element, harmonic sound, aroma, symbol, person, rune, astrological sign, Tarot card, angel, and stone, so there are numerous ways to experience and learn this system of healing magick.

0-87542-890-8, 592 pgs., 7 x 10, illus., softcover $17.95

ANIMAL-SPEAK
The Spiritual & Magical
Powers of Creatures Great & Small
by Ted Andrews

The animal world has much to teach us. Some are experts at survival and adaptation, some never get cancer, some embody strength and courage while others exude playfulness. Animals remind us of the potential we can unfold, but before we can learn from them, we must first be able to speak with them.

Now, for perhaps the first time ever, myth and fact are combined in a manner that will teach you how to speak and understand the language of the animals in your life. *Animal-Speak* helps you meet and work with animals as totems and spirits—by learning the language of their behaviors within the physical world. It provides techniques for reading signs and omens in nature so you can open to higher perceptions and even prophecy. It reveals the hidden, mythical and realistic roles of 45 animals, 60 birds, 8 insects and 6 reptiles.

Animals will become a part of you, revealing to you the majesty and divine in all life. They will restore your childlike wonder of the world and strengthen your belief in magic, dreams and possibilities.

0-87542-028-1, 400 pgs., 7 x 10, illus., photos, sftcvr. $16.00

SHAMANISM AND THE ESOTERIC TRADITION
by Angelique S. Cook & G.A. Hawk

Recharge and enhance your magical practice by returning to the *source* of the entire esoteric tradition—the shamanism of the ancient hunters and gatherers.

Whether you're involved in yoga, divination, or ritual magic, *Shamanism and the Esoteric Tradition* introduces you to the fundamental neo-shamanic techniques that produce immediate results. Shamanic practice is a tremendous aid in self-healing and personal growth. It also produces euphoria by releasing beta-endorphins, an effective antidote against depression.

The enormously powerful techniques presented here include inner journeys to find a power animal and teacher, past-life regression, healing methods, and journeys to help the dead. Gradually and properly used, shamanic power helps you generate positive synchronicities that can alter so-called "chance" life events, and enhance personal satisfaction, freedom and wholeness.

0-87542-325-6, 224 pgs., 6 x 9, illus., index, sftcvr. $12.95

SHAMANISM AND THE MYSTERY LINES
Ley Lines, Spirit Paths, Shape-Shifting & Out-of-Body Travel
by Paul Devereux

This book will take you across archaic landscapes, into contact with spiritual traditions as old as the human central nervous system and into the deepest recesses of the human psyche. Explore the mystery surrounding "ley lines": stone rows, prehistoric linear earthwork, and straight tracks in archaic landscapes around the world. Why would the ancients, without the wheel or horse, want such broad and exact roads? Why the apparent obsession with straightness? Why the parallel sections?

Are they energy lines? Traders' tracks? For those who have definite ideas as to what a ley line is, be prepared for a surprise . . . and a possible shift in your beliefs about this intriguing phenomenon.

The theory put forth and proved in *Shamanism and the Mystery Lines* is startling: that all ancient landscape lines— whether physical manifestations as created by the Amerindians or conceptual as in the case of Feng shui—are in essence *spirit lines.* And underlying the concept of spirit and straightness is a deep, universal experience yielded by the human central nervous system: that of shamanic magical flight—or the out-of-body experience. This explanation is as simple and direct as the lines themselves . . . flight is the straight way over land.

0-87542-189-X, 240 pgs., 6 x 9, illus., softcover $12.95

DANCE OF POWER
A Shamanic Journey
by Dr. Susan Gregg

Join Dr. Susan Gregg on her fascinating, real-life journey to find her soul. This is the story of her shamanic apprenticeship with a man named Miguel, a Mexican-Indian Shaman, or "Nagual." As you live the author's personal experiences, you have the opportunity to take a quantum leap along the path toward personal freedom, toward finding your true self, and grasping the ultimate personal freedom—the freedom to choose moment by moment what you want to experience.

Here, in a warm and genuine style, Dr. Gregg details her studies with Miguel, her travel to other realms, and her initiations by fire and water into the life of a "warrior." If you want to understand how you create your own reality—and how you may be wasting energy by resisting change or trying to understand the unknowable—take the enlightening path of the Nagual.

Practical exercises at the end of each chapter give you the tools to embark upon your own spiritual quest. Learn about another way of being ... *Dance of Power* can change your life, if you let it.

0-87542-247-0, 5¼ x 8, illus., photos, softbound